2nd Grade Suggest(ed) Reading List

Adler, David
Cam Jansen and
the Mystery of the
Dinosaur Bones

Barracca, Debra
The Adventures of Taxi
Dog

Berenstain, Stan & Jan
The Berenstain Bears
books

Bond, Michael
Paddington Bear series

Byars, Betsy Cromer
The chapter books

Caudill, Rebecca
A Pocketful of Cricket

Coerr, Eleanor
Chang's Paper Pony

Cole, Joanna
Big Goof and Little
Goof

Cushman, Doug
Aunt Eater's Mystery
Vacation

Delton, Judy
Pee Wee Scout books

Flack, Marjorie
Story about Ping

**The Funny Side Up
books**
Dinosaur Jokes
Knock, Knock Jokes
School Jokes
Space Jokes
Sports Jokes

Gackenbach, Di(ck)
Mag the Magni(...)

Griffith, Helen V.
Alex and the Cat

Hoban, Lillian
Arthur books

Hoff, Syd
The Horse in Harry's
Room

Holabird, Katherine
Angelina Ballerina

Honeycutt, Natalie
The All New Jonah Twist

Keats, Ezra Jack
Maggie and the Pirate

Kessler, Leonard P.
Here Comes the
Strikeout

Kimmel, Eric A.
The Chanukkah Guest

Komaiko, Leah
Annie Bananie

Kuskin, Karla
Soap Soup

Lexau, Joan M.
Striped Ice Cream

Mayer, Mercer
Just Me books

McCully, Emily Arnold
Zaza's Big Break

McDermott, Gerald
The Stonecutter

O'Connor, Jane
Super Cluck

Pickett, Anola
Old Enough for Magic

Platt, Kin
Big Max

Rey, H. A.
The Curious George
series

Schwartz, Alvin
• Busy Buzzing
Bumblebees and Other
Tongue Twisters
• There Is a Carrot
in My Ear and Other
Noodle Tales
• All of Our Noses Are
Here and Other Noodle
Tales

**Sharmat, Majorie
Weinman**
Big Fat Enormous Lie

Sharmat, Mitchell
Gregory, the Terrible
Eater

Small, David
Imogene's Antlers

Steig, William
The Zabajaba Jungle

Titus, Eve
Anatole books

Zion, Gene
Harry by the Sea

Two

Two living things, blowing in the wind …
One barely moved, the other could bend.

One strongly rooted in the ground, growing tall.
The other, look closely, the blade is so small.

Both are so beautiful, Mother Nature's gift.
One you might climb, one you could lift.

Green is their color, brought on by the spring.
Leaves or blades, they both make me sing!

4

About
Skill Builders
Reading

by R.B. Snow and Ruby Klenk

Welcome to Rainbow Bridge Publishing's Skill Builders series. Like our Summer Bridge Activities™ collection, the Skill Builders series is designed to make learning both fun and rewarding.

This workbook holds students' interest with the right mix of humor, imagination and instruction as they steadily improve their reading comprehension and other skills. The diverse assignments enhance reading skills while giving students something fun to think about—from pumpkins to pets. As students complete the workbook, they will enhance their reading comprehension.

A critical thinking section includes exercises to help develop higher-order thinking skills.

Learning is more effective when approached with an element of fun and enthusiasm—just as most children approach life. That's why the Skill Builders combine entertaining and academically sound exercises with eye-catching graphics and fun themes—to make reviewing basic skills at school or home fun and effective, for both you and your budding scholars.

Table of Contents

1. What two things is this poem comparing?
    A. trees and swings
    B. trees and grass
    C. flowers and grass

2. What color are both things?
    A. yellow
    B. blue
    C. green

3. Write the word from the poem that rhymes with each of these words.

tall   _____

gift   _____

sing   _____

4. Do you think the poet likes the things she is writing about? Why?

_____

_____

_____

_____

Firefly

A little light is going by,
is going up to see the sky,
a little light with wings.

I never would have thought it,
to have a little bug all lit,
and made to go on wings.

—Author Unknown

1. What is this poem about?
   A. the stars in the sky
   B. fireflies
   C. bugs with wings

2. Write down the two pairs of rhyming words in this poem.

   _____   _____

   _____   _____

3. Who is the author of this poem?
   A. Jane Doe
   B. We don't know.
   C. Kim Carlson

4. Have you ever seen a firefly? Draw one below.

Tulips

In my flower garden, <u>tulips</u> always grow,
Straight like toy soldiers all in a row.

With colors so bright, reds, oranges, yellows, too,
They are one of nature's special gifts just for you.

Their colorful petals, shaped like a cup,
Hold the little raindrops for birds to drink up.

Winds cause them to <u>sway,</u>
Back and forth each day.

But still my tulips grow
Like toy soldiers in a row.

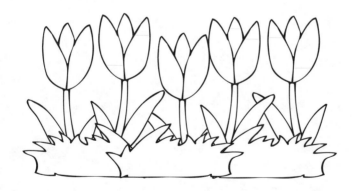

1. What is a <u>tulip</u>?
   A. a soldier
   B. a cup
   C. a flower
   D. a swing

2. How do tulips grow in this poem?
   A. slowly
   B. like soldiers in a row
   C. all over the place

3. Match the rhyming words in this poem.
   grow   up
   day   row
   cup   too
   you   sway

4. What does <u>sway</u> mean?
   A. move up and down
   B. move side to side
   C. stand still

5. Which word from the poem is a compound word?

   _____

Pitter patter, pitter pat …
How I love the rain!

Storm clouds moving in,
The rain is about to begin.
How I love to see the rain!

Tiny sprinkles on my face,
Little droplets playing chase.
How I love to feel the rain!

I open up my mouth so wide,
Letting little drops inside.
How I love to taste the rain!

Tapping on my window,
It's a rhythm that I know.
How I love to hear the rain!

Everything looks so green,
And the fresh air smells so clean.
How I love to smell the rain!

Pitter patter, pitter pat …
How I love the rain!

1. Draw a line from the sense to what the writer of the poem loves about the rain.

sight	fresh air
touch	storm clouds moving in
taste	little drops inside my mouth
sound	tiny sprinkles on my face
smell	tapping on the window

2. Circle the word(s) below that are adverbs. Underline the adjectives.

slowly   quietly

fresh   beautiful

gently   roughly

3. What goes "pitter patter"?
A. feet
B. raindrops
C. clouds

4. Why does the air smell so clean in this poem?

_____

5. Do you like the rain? Why?

_____

_____

The Snowman

It was a snowy day. Braxton and Hayden decided to make a snowman. They bundled up and ran outside. First, they rolled a great big snowball for the body. Then they rolled a medium-sized snowball for the middle. Finally, they rolled a small snowball for the head. They stacked the three snowballs together. They found rocks for his eyes and mouth. They found a pinecone for his nose. They used sticks for his arms. They were proud of their snowman when they finished.

12

Reading Comprehension

1. What was the first thing Braxton and Hayden did?
    A. They found a pinecone for the snowman.
    B. They rolled a great big snowball for the body.
    C. They bundled up and ran outside.
    D. They found rocks for the eyes and mouth.

2. What did Braxton and Hayden use for the snowman's nose?
    A. a pinecone
    B. sticks
    C. a rock

3. What is a compound word?
    A. two words put together to make a new word
    B. a word that describes an action
    C. a word that is used to name things

4. Circle all the compound words you can find in this story.

5. What would you name this snowman?

_____

©RBP Books

My Dog, Eli

My dog, Eli, loves to go to the river. Every Saturday morning I take Eli to the park by the river to play. The first thing Eli does when we get there is run down to the water.

Eli likes to take a drink and splash around. The cold water doesn't bother him. When he gets out of the water, he shakes and shakes. I stand back so all the water doesn't get on me. Then he looks for a rock in the sun to take a nap on. He sleeps there until I whistle for him that it is time to go home.

I think our Saturday trips to the river are something that Eli looks forward to all week.

©RBP Books

Reading Comprehension

1. What is the first thing that Eli does when he gets to the river?

A. He sleeps under a rock.

B. He runs down to the water.

C. He takes a drink of water.

2. Where does Eli take a nap?

A. on my lap

B. on the grass

C. on a rock

D. in the shade

3. Circle the words with short vowel sounds. Underline the words with long vowel sounds.

Eli   splash

week   water

sleeps   in

likes   sun

4. How do you know when dogs are happy?

_____

_____

_____

The Swing

How do you like to go up in a swing,
Up in the air so blue?
Oh, I do think it the pleasantest thing
Ever a child can do!

Up in the air and over the wall,
Till I can see so wide,
Rivers and trees and cattle and all
Over the countryside—

Till I look down on the garden green,
Down on the roof so brown—
Up in the air I go flying again,
Up in the air and down!

Robert Louis Stevenson

www.summerbridgeactivities.com

1. Name three things the child sees when he goes up in the swing.

_____

_____

_____

2. Draw lines between the rhyming pairs of words.

down	do
blue	swing
all	brown
thing	wall

3. Describe what you see when you go up high in a swing.

_____

_____

4. List the things that you see that are the same or different from the things named in the poem.

Same   Different

_____   _____

_____   _____

_____   _____

_____   _____

Every October, Mrs. Lee's class takes a field trip to the pumpkin farm. They walk around the barnyard and through the barn. They see some animals. Then they go for a hayride. A big tractor pulls a large cart of hay. On the hayride, they ride through the apple orchard where the workers are picking apples. Later they will make applesauce. After the hayride, the students go to the pumpkin patch. There are hundreds of pumpkins. Each student picks out a pumpkin to take home. It is always one of the most fun days of the year.

1. Why are the workers picking apples on this farm?
A. to make applesauce
B. to sell at the market
C. to make pies to eat

2. Underline the words below with short vowel sounds.
Circle the words with long vowel sounds.

Lee   trip   apples   patch

pumpkin   hay   ride   after

3. Use the underlined words to make a compound word
to complete the sentence.

A <u>ride</u> in the <u>hay</u> is called a

_____.

A <u>sauce</u> made of <u>apples</u> is called

_____.

The <u>yard</u> around a <u>barn</u> is called a

_____.

4. List things that you can do with pumpkins. Draw your
favorite thing from the list.

_____

Sing a Song of Summer

Sing a song of summer,
My arms stretched open wide.
I run in the sunshine.
I play all day outside.

Hold on to the summer
as long as you may.
Fall will come quickly
and shorten the day.

So play in the water,
roll in the grass.
It won't be long now
before you'll be in class.

1. What season is this poem about?
    A. summer
    B. spring
    C. fall
    D. winter

2. What season will come quickly?
    A. summer
    B. spring
    C. fall
    D. winter

3. There are eight words in this poem with two syllables.
    Can you find them all? Write them down here.

    _____

    _____

    _____

4. Write down the word from the poem that rhymes with
    each word below.

    day _____

    grass _____

    wide _____

The Koala

Have you seen a koala? Koalas live in Australia. They eat leaves from a eucalyptus tree all day long. They may eat more than three pounds of leaves in one day! Many people think that koalas are bears, but they are not. Koalas are marsupials. Marsupials are a special kind of mammal. Marsupials have a pouch on them where their babies go to stay warm and safe. You might be able to see a koala in your local zoo.

Reading Comprehension

1. Where do koalas live?
   A. in Africa
   B. in Australia
   C. in your neighborhood

2. What do koalas eat?
   A. eucalyptus leaves
   B. trees
   C. hamburgers
   D. walnuts
   E. maple leaves

3. Mark the sentences that are true with a T. Mark the sentences that are false with an F.

   _____Fish are mammals.

   _____Marsupials have a pouch to keep their young safe.

   _____Koalas don't eat many leaves.

   _____Koalas are bears.

4. What other animals can you think of that are marsupials? Ask your parents for help if you need to.

   _____

   _____

©RBP Books   Reading Grade 2—RBP3950

Teddy

Mom and Dad think I'm too old to still have my teddy bear. They said, "You are eight years old now, and Teddy shows too much wear." Because I am a big kid, I said OK. I put Teddy up in the closet to hide (but I hung my head).

That night, there was a storm. It was very noisy. I tried and tried but couldn't fall asleep. So I took my Teddy out of his hiding place, and he crawled in bed with me. I did not need him to fall asleep. I just knew he was afraid.

1. Why do the parents ask the child to put Teddy away?
   A. They think Teddy is silly.
   B. They think the child will want to play with other toys instead.
   C. They think the child will lose the bear.
   D. They think the child is too old to have a teddy bear.

2. Why couldn't the child fall asleep?
   A. The storm was too loud.
   B. She wanted to stay awake.
   C. She didn't want to have bad dreams.

3. What did the child do when she couldn't sleep?
   A. She got her teddy bear.
   B. She called for Mom and Dad.
   C. She read a story.

4. Who do you think was really afraid in this story? What made her feel better?

   _____

   _____

The Swamp

In the jungle there was a swamp.

Five wild pigs tromped by. "It's hot," they squealed. So into the swamp they went.

Four monkeys came swinging by. "It's hot," they chattered. So into the swamp they went.

Three frogs hopped by. "It's hot," they croaked. So into the swamp they went.

Two snakes slithered by. "It's hot," they hissed. So into the swamp they went.

One big alligator wriggled by. "It's not hot," he grinned, showing his great big teeth, "but I am hungry." So into the swamp he went.

Suddenly out from the swamp came two snakes, three frogs, four monkeys, and five wild pigs. It didn't feel so hot anymore!

www.summerbridgeactivities.com   ©RBP Books

1. Why did the animals get out of the swamp?
   A. So the alligator would not eat them.
   B. It was too full.
   C. They weren't hot anymore.

2. Draw a line from the animal to the word that describes
   how it talked in this story.
   pigs   croaked
   monkeys   hissed
   frogs   chattered
   snakes   squealed

3. Write T for true and F for false.

   ____ The alligator was hot.   ____ The alligator was hungry.

   ____ The frogs were hot.   ____ The monkeys were hot.

   ____ The snake was hungry.   ____ There were five wild pigs.

4. Write down the animals in the order they appeared in
   the story.

   1. _____   4. _____

   2. _____   5. _____

   3. _____

Tippy

Our family lived on a small farm in the country. We had a dog named Tippy. Tippy was a good dog. He belonged to my brother, Buddy. Tippy followed Buddy everywhere. Buddy taught Tippy to fetch and to do other tricks.

One day, Buddy was hot and tired. He fell asleep by the road. Tippy stayed with him. When a car came by, Tippy ran to the car and barked. He barked and barked until the driver of the car saw Buddy. The driver stopped. He woke Buddy up. He took Buddy down the lane to our mom. Tippy saved Buddy's life.

1. What is the main idea of this story?
   A. a dog saves a boy
   B. a dog learns new tricks
   C. life in the country
   D. don't play in the road

2. What did Buddy teach Tippy to do?
   A. to chase cars
   B. to fetch and other tricks
   C. to bark at cars
   D. to run in circles

3. Where did Buddy fall asleep?
   A. in a sleeping bag
   B. in his bed
   C. in his mother's bed
   D. by the road

4. How did Tippy save Buddy's life?
   A. pulled him out of the road
   B. barked at a car until it stopped
   C. ran to Buddy's mom
   D. got a policeman

Playing in the Park

My brother and I like to play in the park by my grand-mother's house. Grandmother takes us for walks to the park. My brother goes down the small slide. I slide down the big slide. He climbs on the small bars. I climb the big tower. I twirl on the tire swing. He swings on the baby swing. I swing across the tricky bars. He walks on a little board. We both like to climb the climbing wall. Sometimes we play ball with friends we meet at the park. Other times we play tag. When we get hungry, we have a picnic. We always have a great time at the park with Grandmother.

1. What is the main idea of this story?
   A. going down the slide
   B. playing on the swings
   C. playing in the park
   D. making friends in the park

2. Who takes the children to the park?
   A. grandmother
   B. sister
   C. father
   D. mother

3. Who goes down the small slide?
   A. sister
   B. little brother
   C. big brother
   D. the friend

4. You can probably tell that—
   A. both children are the same age
   B. the children fight
   C. the children don't like to go to the park
   D. one child is older than the other

Insects can be many different shapes and sizes. But all insects have some things in common. All insects have three main body parts. They have a head, a body that is called a <u>thorax</u>, and an abdomen. All insects have six legs. Most insects have feelers on their head called antennae. Many insects use their antennae to see, taste, and hear.

1. How many legs does an insect have?
   A. six
   B. eight
   C. four

2. What is a <u>thorax</u>?
   A. abdomen
   B. body
   C. leg
   D. antennae

3. Write T for true and F for false for the following sentences.

   _____ All insects have nine legs.

   _____ All insects have an abdomen.

   _____ Bugs come in different sizes.

4. What do insects use their antennae for?
   A. to greet other insects
   B. to see, taste, and hear
   C. to dance

Opposites

My brother and I are opposites.
Believe me because it's true.

I have brown eyes, but
My brother's eyes are blue.

When I sit, my brother stands.
I sunburn easily, but he tans.

I am quiet. He is loud.
I am humble. He is proud.

I like soft music. He likes rock.
I like to sing. He likes to talk.

Although we're opposites to the end,
My brother still is my best friend.

www.summerbridgeactivities.com

1. What is the main idea?
   A. It's okay to be different.
   B. Even though the brothers are different, they are still best friends.
   C. The brother has blue eyes and tans well.

2. Write down the opposite of these words.

brother _____

sit _____

loud _____

proud _____

3. What is a synonym for <u>humble</u>?
   A. proud
   B. discreet
   C. modest

4. How are you and your best friend different? How are you the same?

_____

_____

_____

The Library

Behind my door, adventures are free,
so open it quietly and come to me.
I am a library and through my door
are shelves and shelves of books <u>galore</u>.
Books will take you anywhere;
just open the cover and you'll be there.
They take you to the sky or outer space,
into the ocean, a deep, deep place.
They can take you to beaches with the whitest sands,
or to long-ago times or <u>distant lands</u>.
Read the open books to see
what the world can really be!

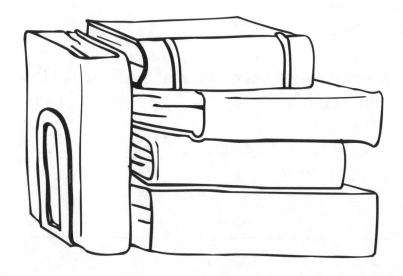

©RBP Books

1. What is the main idea of this story?

A. The library is a great place to go for adventure.

B. The ocean is a deep place.

C. The library has a lot of books.

2. <u>Distant lands</u> means

A. next door

B. faraway places

C. nowhere

3. What does <u>galore</u> mean in this poem?

A. a lot

B. a few

C. some

4. How can books take you anywhere?

_____

_____

_____

_____

_____

A Song for My Son

Here's a song for my son. It's a <u>hymn</u> for him. It's about the day my poor son rode away. My son rode on his bike down the road in the sun. He rode and he rode down the road. He rode for a week until his knees felt weak. Then he pressed on his brake to take a break. He ate eight pairs of pears. Then he blew a big blue bubble. That night as the sun set, my son became a knight, and I never saw my son again.

© RBP Books

1. What is a <u>hymn</u>?
   A. a story
   B. a song
   C. a poem

2. What did the son eat?
   A. eight pairs of pears
   B. a pear of pairs
   C. eight pear of pairs
   D. a pair of pears

3. Circle the correct homonym in each sentence.

The boys (ate, eight) everyone's dessert.

The (sun, son) rises in the east.

The sky is (blew, blue).

I have a new (pair, pear) of pants.

4. Write a homonym for each word below.

hymn _____   ate _____

sun _____   pair _____

week _____   blew _____

brake _____   night _____

The Gigantic Cookie

My mother baked a <u>gigantic</u> cookie for me. I sat on my porch to eat it. But before I took a bite, my friend Anna came by.

"Will you share your cookie with me?" Anna asked. So I broke my cookie into two pieces, one for me and one for Anna. But before we took a bite, Jesse and Lucy came by.

"Will you share your cookie with us?" they asked. So Anna and I each broke our cookie pieces into two pieces. Now we had four pieces, one for me, one for Anna, one for Jesse, and one for Lucy. But before we took a bite, four more friends came by.

"Will you share your cookie with us?" they asked. So Anna, Jesse, Lucy, and I all broke our pieces in half. Now we had enough to share with eight friends. But before we took a bite, eight more friends came by.

"Will you share your cookie with us?" they asked. We all broke our pieces in half to share with our eight new friends. I looked at my gigantic cookie. It was no longer gigantic.

"Hey, anyone know what is gigantic when there's one, but small when there are sixteen?" I said.

"No, what?" my friends asked.

"My cookie," I laughed.

www.summerbridgeactivities.com

©RBP Books

1. What happened in this story?

A. Sixteen people shared the cookie.

B. Mom bought a gigantic cookie.

C. The cookie was terrible.

2. Number the sentences in the order they happened in the story.

_____ Jesse and Lucy came by.

_____ Mother baked a cookie.

_____ Four friends came by.

_____ Anna came by.

_____ Eight friends came by.

3. What does <u>gigantic</u> mean?

A. small

B. huge

C. tiny

D. fat

4. Whom would you share your cookie with?

_____

"Happy Mother's Day," Nathan said. Nathan gave his mother a large box with a pretty bow.

"What is it?" his mother asked.

"You have to guess," Nathan said. "I'll give you a hint. It's soft and blue."

"Can I wear it?" asked his mother.

"Yes," said Nathan.

"I think I know," his mother said.

She opened the box. "Thank you. It is just what I asked for," she said.

Nathan's mother took the gift out of the box. She put it on over her head. She put her arms in the sleeves. It fit just right. Nathan's mother gave him a big hug.

1. What did Nathan's mother receive?
A. a necklace
B. a sweater
C. a scarf

2. Why did Nathan give his mother a gift?
A. It was her birthday.
B. It was Mother's Day.
C. It was Christmas.

3. The words <u>it</u>, <u>she</u>, and <u>he</u> take the place of a person or thing in the story. Answer the questions below.

He gave her a large box. Who is <u>he</u>?

_____

She opened the box. Who is <u>she</u>?

_____

She put it on over her head. What is <u>it</u>?

_____

4. Draw a picture of the present that Nathan gave his mother.

"Please, Mom. Please may I have a pet of my own?" asked Jackie. "Well, you have shown that you can be <u>responsible</u>. I guess it's time you had your own pet," said Mother. "Hurray! Let's go!" shouted Jackie.

"But first you need to think about the right pet," said Mother. "The right pet? I don't understand," said Jackie. "The right pet is the right size. The right pet is the right one for you. You need to think about where you will keep your pet. You need to think about how much time you have to take care of it," explained Mother.

"Well," said Jackie. "We live in an apartment, so I guess it will need to be small. I want a pet that I can hold. I want a pet that I can <u>cuddle</u> with."

"Now you're thinking," said Mother. "Let's go see what we can find."

Jackie and her mom went to the pet store. Jackie said to the pet store owner, "I am looking for a small, furry pet that I can hold." The pet store owner showed Jackie a puppy. The puppy was small and furry. But Jackie knew it wouldn't always be small and furry. It would grow up to be a big dog. Jackie looked at a goldfish. "No good," she said. "I can't hold it." Finally, Jackie saw a gerbil. "This is perfect. It is small. I can hold it. It has fur. I can cuddle with it. This is the right pet for me," said Jackie. Jackie took the pet home. Now Jackie's only problem is deciding on just the right name for just the right pet.

1. What does <u>responsible</u> mean in this story?
A. to remember to feed and clean the pet and its cage
B. to remember only to feed the pet
C. to feed and clean the pet when you remember

2. Which of the following are pets? Put an X next to them.

_____ elephant   _____ giraffe

_____ parrot   _____ turtle

_____ gerbil   _____ kangaroo

_____ gorilla   _____ cat

_____ rabbit   _____ mouse

3. Why didn't Jackie want a goldfish?
A. She doesn't like to swim.
B. She wanted a pet she could hold.
C. The fish wouldn't talk to her.

4. What does <u>cuddle</u> mean?
A. to hold and hug
B. to play with
C. to jump with

Reading Grade 2—RBP3950

Pet Show

Today is the day of the neighborhood pet show. Holly, Amanda, Nico, and Nathan have brought their pets. See if you can match the children to their pets.

Nathan's pet likes to chase the girl's cat.
Holly's pet sings from its perch.
Nico's pet runs around on a wheel in its cage.

Put an X in the box when you know an animal does not belong to a child. Put an O when you know an animal does belong.

	Cat	Dog	Hamster	Bird
Holly				
Amanda				
Nico				
Nathan				

Reading Comprehension

1. Who brought their pets?

_____   _____

_____   _____

2. List all the animals in this story.

_____   _____

_____   _____

3. Match the children with the pet they brought.

Holly   bird
Amanda   cat
Nico   dog
Nathan   hamster

4. Which of these animals would you like best for a pet?
Why?

_____

_____

_____

_____

My Pet Lamb

I have a pet lamb. She is little. Her mom cannot take care of her, so I do! I use a baby bottle to feed her warm milk. She sleeps in the barn on soft clean hay. She sleeps a lot.

I named my pet lamb Cotton because she is soft and white. I keep her clean by giving her a bath with warm water and a soft rag every day. She doesn't like having her face and ears washed.

When the sun is shining we go for walks down in the field. Cotton likes to run all around the field, smell the flowers, and watch the butterflies.

I try to play tag with her. Most of the time she just wants to run after me. We have fun running around.

When we get tired of playing, we lie out in the sun and take a short nap. I think she knows that I'm her best friend. I know that I really love her!

©RBP Books

1. What adjectives are used to describe Cotton?
   A. small and funny
   B. short and cute
   C. soft and white

2. What does Cotton <u>not</u> like?
   A. having her ears and face washed
   B. playing in the fields
   C. sleeping in the sun

3. Write T for true sentences and F for false sentences.

   _____ Cotton is a lamb.

   _____ A lamb is a baby moose.

   _____ Cotton likes to eat dandelions.

   _____ Cotton likes to watch butterflies.

   _____ Cotton likes to sleep in the rain.

   _____ Cotton doesn't like to run.

4. Complete these words by writing the ending.

   slee_____   bott_____   wash_____

   arou_____   playi_____   flowe_____

5. Can you find the compound words in this story?
   Circle them. (Hint: There are two of them.)

©RBP Books   Reading Grade 2—RBP3950

Marvin the Moose

Marvin was a happy moose. He lived in the woods near Bar Harbor, Maine. Summer was Marvin's favorite time of year. From his mountain he watched the tourists biking and the sailboats sailing into the harbor.

Marvin spent most of his time alone. Marvin was very curious about the tourists, however. He <u>longed</u> to look into the shop windows and walk to the pier.

Marvin knew that it was unsafe to wander into town in broad daylight, so he decided to go at night. That night, Marvin walked to Bar Harbor. He peeked into the ice cream shop. He crept past the jewelry store. Before he knew it, Marvin had walked right onto the pier. Marvin enjoyed the beautiful Atlantic Ocean. He thought he saw a whale.

Marvin was tired. He decided he had better head back home. Slowly, Marvin went back up the mountain and into the woods.

Marvin was very proud of himself for being so sneaky. "I walked all through town, and no one saw me!" Marvin thought. The next morning, the newspaper headlines read: "Moose Wanders Bar Harbor!" Guess whose picture was on the front page!

1. How does this story end?

    A. Someone saw Marvin and wrote about it.

    B. Marvin goes home alone.

    C. The tourists ask Marvin to leave.

2. What is a synonym for <u>longed</u> in this story?

    A. wished

    B. cried

    C. waited

3. Why was summer Marvin's favorite time of year?

    A. He could watch the whales.

    B. He could go biking.

    C. He could watch the tourists and the sailboats.

4. Who do you suppose saw Marvin?

_____

_____

51

How to Frost a Cake

Jessica is making a cake for her mother's birthday. Her grandmother helped her bake the cake. But her grandmother had to go home. She left the following directions for Jessica.

1. Remove the cake from the baking pan and put it on a plate. To do this, place a plate face down on the cake. Then flip the cake and the plate over. Remove the baking pan.

2. Open the frosting can. Spoon some frosting onto the middle of the cake.

3. Spread the frosting using the spreader. Always work from the center out to the sides. Add more frosting as needed. Spread the frosting evenly over all of the cake.

Be careful not to press too hard, or you will tear the cake.

1. What is the cake for?
   A. Grandmother's birthday
   B. a Christmas party
   C. Mother's birthday

2. What comes last?
   A. Spread the frosting evenly over all of the cake.
   B. Remove the cake from the baking pan.
   C. Spoon some frosting onto the middle of the cake.

3. What warning did Grandma give Jessica?
   A. Don't lick your fingers.
   B. Don't use too much frosting.
   C. Don't share the cake with anyone.
   D. Be careful not to press too hard.

4. What is your favorite kind of cake? Draw a picture of it.

_____

Riding a Rainbow

Nickolas would not go to sleep at night. Every night he would ask his mom, "Can't I just stay up a little longer?" One night, his mom asked him, "Why do you never want to sleep?" Nickolas answered, "Because I am afraid I will miss something!"

His mom laughed at that. "Don't you know that by staying up late you are missing out on the most fun of all?" she asked.

"I am?" Nickolas said.

"When you are sleeping, there is no limit to what you can do!" his mom said. "You can ride a rainbow on the back of a golden unicorn. You can talk to a leprechaun. You can travel through kingdoms and tell all the dragons to brush their teeth! You can fly a plane or swim in the ocean. You can make monsters your best friends or marry a princess! You can do anything you want to in your sleep, and the best part is you wake up right in your own bed every morning no matter what!"

Nickolas thought about what his mom had told him. He thought about it all day long. Nickolas was <u>skeptical</u> about his mom's idea. He wasn't sure it would work. That night, he thought he would try it. Nickolas went to bed on time.

That night he flew through space, played tic-tac-toe with aliens, and became a famous soccer player.

Now he goes to bed early!

1. What is this story about?

A. Nickolas wants to be a famous soccer player.

B. Going to sleep at night can be fun.

C. Sleeping is bad for you.

2. How does Nickolas get to do all those fun things?

A. by watching television

B. by listening to his mom

C. by dreaming of them

3. This story says that Nickolas was <u>skeptical</u> of his mom's idea. What does that mean?

A. Nickolas didn't understand what his mom said.

B. Nickolas wasn't sure if his mom was right.

C. Nickolas thought it was a great idea.

4. What did you dream about last night? Tell the story below and draw a picture of it.

_____

_____

_____

The Birthday Present Mix-up

Today is Rachel's birthday. She invited four friends to her party. Each friend brought a present. Rachel's little brother mixed up the tags on the presents. Can you use the clues to put the tags on the right presents?

Kelly's present has flowered wrapping paper and a bow.
Kate's present is square and has a bow.
Meg forgot the bow on her present.
Lisa's present has striped wrapping paper.

Put an X in the box when you know a present does not belong to one of the girls. Put an O when you know a present belongs to one of the girls.

	Square, striped with bow	Square, flowered with bow	Square, flowered without bow	Rectangle, striped with bow
Kate				
Kelly				
Lisa				
Meg				

56

1. Whose party is this?
   A. Rachel's birthday party
   B. Kelly's birthday party
   C. Meg's birthday party
   D. Lisa's birthday party

2. Whose present doesn't have a bow?
   A. Lisa's
   B. Meg's
   C. Rachel's
   D. Kate's

3. Who didn't bring a present?
   A. Lisa
   B. Kate
   C. Kelly
   D. Rachel
   E. Meg

4. What do you think is inside each present? Draw a picture of each thing.

Who's My Pen Pal?

For one year I have been writing to a <u>pen pal</u>. A pen pal is a friend that you write to. My pen pal's name is Max. He is in the second grade. He lives in Canada with his family. Today Max is coming for a visit. I am going to meet him at the airport. I have never seen Max, so I'm not sure what he looks like. Max said to look for a boy with curly hair and glasses. Max said he would be wearing a baseball cap and carrying a backpack. Can you help me find Max?

1. Color in Max on the previous page.

2. Why doesn't the writer know what Max looks like?
A. He forgot.
B. He has never seen Max.
C. Max changed his hair color.

3. Write a T next to true sentences and an F next to false sentences.

_____ Max has curly hair.

_____ Max has glasses.

_____ Max lives in the United States.

_____ Max likes to play soccer.

4. What is a <u>pen pal</u>?
A. a cousin that lives far away
B. a person from Canada
C. a friend that you write to
D. someone who gives you a pen

Kate and Her Dad

Kate loves doing things with her dad. He is her best friend. Her dad loves to play basketball. Kate plays basketball with her dad. He is the coach of her team. Sometimes after a game, they go to the ice cream store. They both have chocolate ice cream.

After work, Kate and her dad go to the school. They like to run around the track. This helps them stay in shape. Kate and her dad make friends at the track.

At bedtime, Kate curls up on her dad's lap. He reads her bedtime stories. Kate thinks her dad is the greatest.

www.summerbridgeactivities.com

1. What is this story mostly about?
   A. playing ball
   B. things Kate does with her dad
   C. running track
   D. bedtime stories

2. Where do Kate and her dad make friends?
   A. at the park
   B. at the playground
   C. running track
   D. playing basketball

3. Who is the coach of Kate's basketball team?
   A. her brother
   B. a friend
   C. her mother
   D. her dad

4. You can guess that—
   A. Kate and her dad are very close.
   B. her dad is too busy to spend time with her.
   C. they never have fun.
   D. Dad is too tired to play with Kate.

5. Name three things you like to do with your dad or mom.

   _____

   _____

   _____

Compound Fun

Can you find a match? Find all the compound words in the butterflies below by matching the caterpillars to their cocoons. Draw a line between each pair and then to the matching butterfly.

BUTTER + FLY = BUTTERFLY

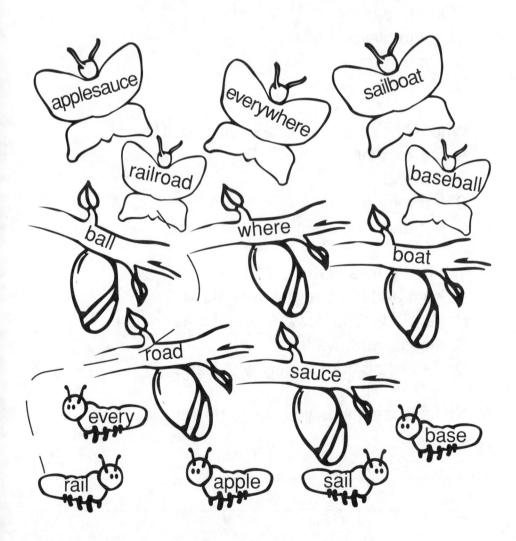

Homonym Puzzle

Homonyms are words that sound the same but can be spelled differently and mean different things. There are six pairs of homonyms in the puzzle below. See if you can find all six.

~~blew~~	weak	see
blue	week	sea
ate	son	pear
eight	sun	pair

```
i  e  m  z  j  v  e  j  g  q
x  r  i  r  p  a  i  r  e  r
t  o  h  g  f  d  p  q  e  j
h  r  a  i  h  e  n  k  e  a
e  u  l  b  a  t  e  q  s  b
z  l  f  r  r  e  s  s  e  l
s  t  n  s  w  y  u  b  m  e
g  e  x  o  s  a  n  r  b  w
x  m  a  n  t  c  l  w  x  h
p  k  a  e  w  r  v  q  a  k
```

Reading Grade 2—RBP3950

Compound Clues

Can you figure out these clues to write the compound word below?

 + = __rainbow__

 + = _____

 + = _____

+ = _____

 + = _____

Can you think of one?

+ = __bookworm__

Map It!

On the following pages you will find a map. Using the clues below, find where on the map the hidden treasure should be. Read the instructions carefully!

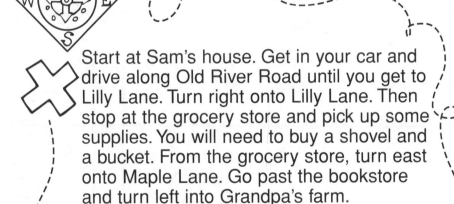

Start at Sam's house. Get in your car and drive along Old River Road until you get to Lilly Lane. Turn right onto Lilly Lane. Then stop at the grocery store and pick up some supplies. You will need to buy a shovel and a bucket. From the grocery store, turn east onto Maple Lane. Go past the bookstore and turn left into Grandpa's farm.

At Grandpa's farm, you will need to get out of your car and take a walk on the foot trail behind his barn. Follow the trail over the river and to the swamp. You will find the treasure buried behind the "No Swimming" sign!

Map It!

Use the map to complete the exercises on pages 65 and 68.

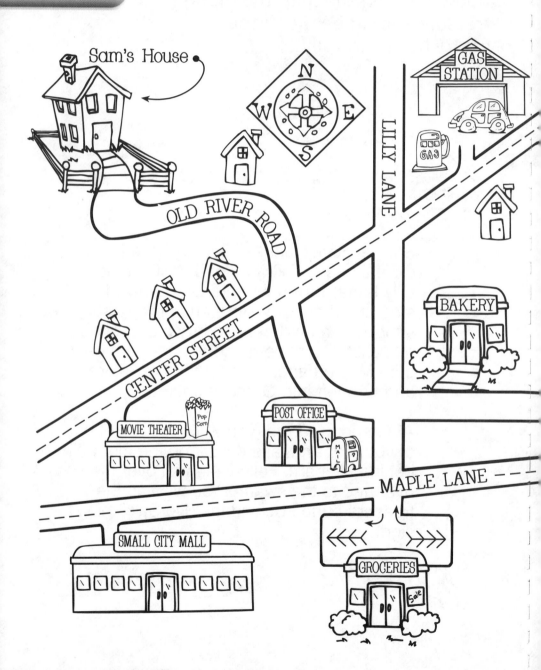

Map It!

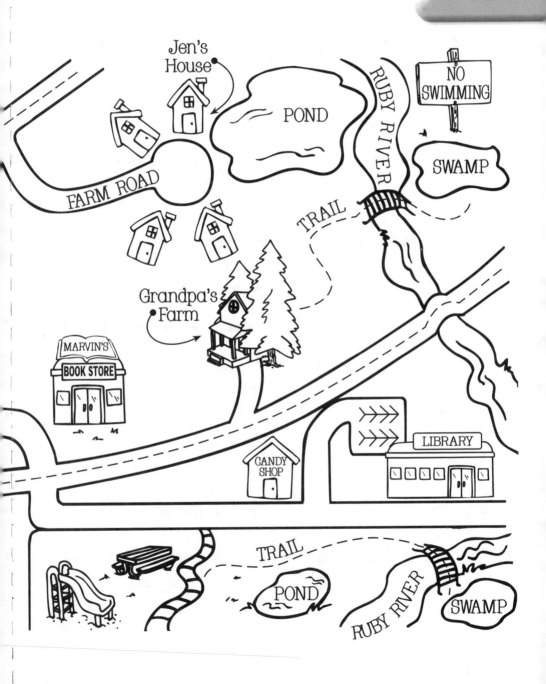

Critical Thinking Skills

1. Using the map on pages 66–67, write down directions to get from Jen's house to the library.

   _____

   _____

   _____

2. Did you have to pass the post office to get to the

   library? _____

3. Did you have to pass the park? _____

4. Which direction were you going while on Lilly Lane?
   A. north
   B. south
   C. east
   D. west

5. Ruby River is to the (west, east) of the bookstore.

6. The park is on the (north, south) side of the map.

Crossword

Complete the crossword puzzle below.

Across

1. homonym for <u>eight</u>
4. A pot of gold is at the end of the _____.
7. synonym for "the same": a ___ ___ ___ ___

Down

1. Birds fly in the _____.
2. opposite of <u>nowhere</u>
3. We watched the _____ on the 4th of July.
5. homonym for <u>blew</u>
6. We are best _____.

Underline the main idea.

John and Matt want to be firemen. They want to ride on the big fire truck. John wants to climb ladders and rescue people from fires. Matt wants to hold the big hose and spray water on the fires to put them out.

A. John and Matt want to be firemen.
B. John wants to climb a ladder.
C. Matt wants to hold a fire hose.

Jenny visited her grandmother in the hospital. She saw how kind and helpful the nurses were to her grandmother. Now she wants to be a nurse when she grows up. She wants to help sick people get well.

A. Jenny got sick.
B. Jenny wants to be a nurse.
C. Her grandmother was in the hospital.

Grandma, Get better soon!

Finding the Main Idea

Underline the main idea.

Mrs. Jones and Mrs. Brown are bakers. They work at a store called Bake Goods to Go. Mrs. Jones works nights. She bakes cakes, cookies, and pies. Mrs. Brown works in the daytime. She bakes bread and rolls. Both Mrs. Jones and Mrs. Brown are very good bakers.

A. Mrs. Jones bakes pies.
B. Mrs. Brown bakes rolls.
C. Mrs. Jones and Mrs. Brown are bakers.

Mary has a new pet. Her pet is a baby kitten. It is soft and cuddly. The kitten likes to sleep a lot. Mary put a soft blanket in a box for its bed. Mary plays with her kitten when it is awake. She never forgets to feed her kitten.

A. The kitten sleeps a lot.
B. Mary plays with her kitten.
C. Mary's new pet is a kitten.

71

Critical Thinking Skills

Write each group of words under the question it answers on page 73.

my best friend

next door

in the gym

rode a skateboard

the builder

my brother

basketball player

at school

will build a house

last night

after lunch

in the closet

made a basket

hid my present

grandmother

today

ate my desert

soon

©RBP Books

Who, What, When, Where

Who?

Did What?

Where?

When?

Answer Pages

Page 5
1. B
2. C
3. small, lift, spring
4.-Answers will vary.

Page 7
1. B
2. by, sky, it, lit
3. B
4. Answers will vary.

Page 9
1. C
2. B
3. grow/row, day/sway, cup/up, you/too
4. B
5. raindrops

Page 11
1. sight/storm clouds moving in, touch/tiny sprinkles on my face, taste/little drops inside my mouth, sound/tapping on the window, smell/fresh air
2. circled: slowly, quietly, roughly, gently; underlined: fresh, beautiful
3. B
4. Answers will vary.
5. Answers will vary.

Page 13
1. C
2. A
3. A
4. snowman, outside, snowball, snowballs, pinecone
5. Answers will vary.

Page 15
1. B
2. C
3. circled: splash, water, in, sun; underlined: Eli, week, sleeps, likes
4. Answers will vary.

Page 17
1. rivers, trees, cattle, garden, roof, wall
2. down/brown, blue/do, all/wall, thing/swing
3. Answers will vary.
4. Answers will vary.

Page 19
1. A
2. underlined: trip, apples, patch, pumpkin, after; circled: Lee, hay, ride
3. hayride, applesauce, barnyard
4. Answers will vary.

Page 21
1. A
2. C
3. summer, open, sunshine, outside, quickly, shorten, water, before
4. may, class, outside

Page 23
1. B
2. A
3. F, T, F, F
4. Answers will vary. (e.g., kangaroo, opossum)

Page 25
1. D
2. A
3. A
4. Answers will vary.

Answer Pages

Page 27
1. A
2. pigs/squealed, monkeys/chattered, frogs/croaked, snakes/hissed
3. left to right: F, T, T, T, F, T
4. pigs, monkeys, frogs, snakes, alligator

Page 29
1. A
2. B
3. D
4. B

Page 31
1. C
2. A
3. B
4. D

Page 33
1. A
2. B
3. F, T, T
4. B

Page 35
1. B
2. sister, stand, quiet, humble
3. C
4. Answers will vary.

Page 37
1. A
2. B
3. A
4. Answers will vary.

Page 39
1. B
2. A
3. ate, sun, blue, pair
4. left to right: him, eight, son, pear, weak, blue, break, knight

Page 41
1. A
2. 3, 1, 4, 2, 5
3. B
4. Answers will vary.

Page 43
1. B
2. B
3. Nathan, Mother, sweater
4. Answers will vary.

Page 45
1. A
2. parrot, turtle, gerbil, cat, rabbit, mouse
3. B
4. A

Page 47
1. Holly, Amanda, Nico, Nathan
2. cat, dog, hamster, bird
3. Holly/bird, Amanda/cat, Nico/hamster, Nathan/dog
4. Answers will vary.

Page 49
1. C
2. A
3. T, F, F, T, F, F
4. sleeps, bottle, washed, around, playing, flowers
5. cannot, butterflies

Page 51
1. A
2. A
3. C
4. Answers will vary.

Answer Pages

Page 53
1. C
2. A
3. D
4. Answers will vary.

Page 55
1. B
2. C
3. B
4. Answers will vary.

Page 57
1. A
2. B
3. D
4. Answers will vary.

Page 59
1. Max is in the top-right corner.
2. B
3. T, T, F, F
4. C

Page 61
1. B
2. C
3. D
4. A
5. Answers will vary.

Page 62

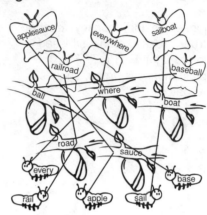

Page 63

Page 64
rainbow, basketball, cornbread, sunglasses, firefly

Answer Pages

Page 68
1. Answers will vary.
2. no
3. yes
4. B
5. east
6. south

Page 69

Across:
1. ate
4. rainbow
7. alike

Down:
1. air
2. everywhere
3. fireworks
5. blue
6. friends

Page 70
1. A
2. B

Page 71
1. C
2. C

Page 72–73
Who?
my best friend
the builder
my brother
basketball player
grandmother

Did What?
rode a skateboard
will build a house
made a basket
hid my present
ate my dessert

When?
last night
after lunch
today
soon

Where?
next door
in the gym
at school
in the closet

Notes

Five things I'm thankful for:

1. _____
2. _____
3. _____
4. _____
5. _____

Notes

Five things I'm thankful for:

1. _____
2. _____
3. _____
4. _____
5. _____

Notes

_____
_____
_____
_____
_____
_____
_____
_____
_____
_____
_____
_____
_____
_____
_____
_____
_____
_____
_____
_____
_____

Five things I'm thankful for:

1. _____
2. _____
3. _____
4. _____
5. _____